EXCUSE ME

I CANNOT COME

Reverend Samuel A. Abegunde

Scripture quotations marked GNB are from Good News Bible
Scripture quotations marked RV are from Revised Standard Version
Scripture quotations marked ASV are from American Standard Version
Scripture quotations marked GW are from God's Word.
Quotations marked KJV are from King James Version.

ISBN: 978-0-9886615-6-1

Liberty Publishers
P.O. Box 18417
Philadelphia, PA 19120

This book is
lovingly
dedicated
To
my wife,

Pastor (Mrs.) Bernice Abegunde

BOOKS BY SAME AUTHOR

Integrity in Ministry
This book is a must read for every Christian Worker – Usher, Choir Director, Deacon, Deaconess, Pastor, Evangelist, Bishop, Archbishop, General Overseer, etc. The cost is $5.00 plus $2.50 for shipping.

Hiring Shepherds, Not Hirelings
This is an informative book in evaluating whether a minister is a hireling or an authentic shepherd, whether he or she is called by God or self-appointed. The book challenges the business minds and money making practices of today's ministers under the pretense of preaching the gospel.

Why Are You Alone?
This book examines the low points in David's life. Readers will learn that traveling the rugged road of life alone without the counsel of God is a recipe for disaster, whereas walking with God brings victorious living without sweat, blood and tears.

The Quiet Life of Isaac

This book is about marriage, raising of children and healthy family relations. Looking from afar, Rebekah and Isaac's marriage looked good and inspiring. As you move closer, you see rivalry, deceit, and a house divided. As you read this book, you will learn of the importance that Christ can make in your marriage and raising children only if you let Him.

The Wounded Man

This book is about the lessons we can learn about human attitudes. The question is: "What is the need in a human being that makes another person exhibit unhealthy attitude?" As you read this book, you will find yourself in some of the attitudes of the characters you are going to read about. You will learn important lessons of love, compassion, and responsibility.

From Gilgal To Jordan

In this book, the journey of a servant is described in four practical stages based in particular on the call and the works of Elisha. However, the journey experiences are specifically applicable to every authentic servant of God. It is very helpful to observe and note how a servant begins his ministry journey and responds to rising challenges during the journey.

TABLE OF CONTENTS

Excuses! Excuses!! Excuses!!!

Somebody once said, "Excuses are tools of the incompetent, and those who specialize in them seldom go far."

Benjamin Franklin wrote, "He that is good for making excuses is seldom good for anything else."

Billy Sunday defined an excuse as, "The skin of a reason stuffed with a lie".

Gabriel Meurier stated, "He who excuses himself, accuses himself."

David Legge in his sermon on excuses said, "Excuses are not reasons. A reason is something that holds weight, a reason is justified, a reason is a plausible thing – why you have not done something – but an excuse is not plausible."

Webster's New World College Dictionary defines excuse as: "to try to free a person of blame; seek to exonerate; to try to minimize or pardon a fault; to consider an offense or fault as not important; a pretended reason for conduct."

Martin Luther King Jr. said, "If a man is called to be a street sweeper, he should sweep streets even as Michelangelo painted or Beethoven played music, or Shakespeare wrote poetry. He should sweep streets so well that all the hosts of heaven and earth will pause to say, here lived a great street-sweeper who did his job well."

Elizabeth Dole said, "It is not what I do that matters, but what a sovereign God chooses to do through me. God does not want worldly successes. He wants my heart in submission to Him."

There is no one too young, too old, too rich, too poor or too busy for God to use. When Abraham was 90 years old, God called him and asked him to walk before him and be perfect. God called Samuel at about age 17. God called Moses at age so though he had a bad record: he was wanted for murder.

To be a disciple of Jesus is a sacrifice. It may cost you your habits, your friends, your favorite life styles. Jesus did not have a home of his own, no bed to sleep on at night, no pillow to make his head comfortable, and no leisure time. Jesus held no title to a car or landed property. He had neither bank account nor suitcase to pack his belongings, changing attire, toothbrush and towel. He wore sandals on the hot sands of Palestine deserts.

ACKNOWLEDGEMENTS

My debts are many, and it would be impossible to list them here. I am grateful to Pastor (Mrs.) Bernice Abegunde for her editorial suggestions and help; most especially her loyal commitment and support for my book project.

I am indebted to Bishop Stanley Webb who, in spite of his busy ministerial job schedule, meticulously reviewed the manuscript, offered constructive suggestions and agreed to write the foreword to this book. His excellent comments on the manuscript and wonderful generous support of this treatise is deeply encouraging. I am indeed grateful to Dr. Akin and Dr. (Mrs.) Kemi Bankole who agreed to proofread and make corrections to this work.

Deep thanks to the authors of the Chain Reference Bible, Life Application Study Bible, other writers and authors cited in this work from whom I have benefited.

FOREWORD

During his many years of Christian experience, education, pastor and counseling ministry, Rev. Samuel Abegunde noticed that the nature of people in their sinful state have not changed since the days of the early church or soon after God made man. So, he systematically, in this book, takes us through the scriptures to authenticate the lesson God has given him to share with us. Even the children of God, who have confessed the Lord Jesus Christ as Savior, often experience the same problems of procrastination and making excuses when they are called to do the work of God.

In this thoughtful presentation, Rev. Abegunde helps you to see how the enemy of God often causes us to procrastinate or make unnecessary excuses, when the assignments are to do the will of God. As you move forward in reading this thoughtful presentation, you will better understand the nature and workings of the enemy, and learn how to defeat him through the indwelling power of the Holy Spirit. You will be able to move ahead with a victorious life and ministry, knowing that you are in the will of God.

"I delight to do thy will, O my God: yea, thy law is within my heart."
Psalm 40:8

Bishop Stanley Webb, MA, D. Min.
New Life Church of God
1034-38 Rising Sun Avenue,
Philadelphia, PA 19140.

INTRODUCTION

THE GALLERY OF EXCUSES

I would like to take you through imagination lane for a few seconds. Imagine yourself sitting in a huge ballroom; in that ballroom you meet Moses, and Moses tells you that Elijah, Jesus, Solomon, Abraham and all those fathers of faith you read about in the Bible, including Deborah, Joshua, Jeremiah, etc. are all in that same ballroom! How proud and happy will you be to be present in that gathering? Will you enjoy seeing them all, and probably take a photograph? Will you probably shake their hands and introduce yourself? That is exactly what will happen on a day appointed by God. Will you be in that room on appointed day?

This book is about silly, flimsy and unreasonable excuses that people give in order to avoid involvement in serving God or going to His house. (Those excuses that will serve as an impediment to prevent many from being in that room that day). This book stands as a warning and a reminder to those who are careless about the life hereafter, which we call eternity. Let us be reminded that Noah must have preached to his generation for a period of time and, not a single soul was won, most likely because he was not taken seriously. Then the flood came according to the warnings of God and wiped that generation off. Again, the wickedness of Sodom was of concern to God; Abraham interceded but Sodom had chosen a path of destruction and the two sister cities of Sodom and Gomorrah perished in the catastrophe.

Having lived in America for decades, I have observed how the meteorologists together with the News Media repeatedly sound the alarm to warn citizens of coming inclement and hazardous weather situations before their arrival, which many heed, prepare for and are therefore protected. Others take warnings and forecast lightly, just don't care, are not prepared and are taken away violently. Some stand out in my memory, such as New Orleans experience with hurricane Katrina on

August 20, 2005, where several who did not prepare and escape to the shelter lost their lives. Hurricane Sandy showed devastation in its path in parts of New York and New Jersey on October 29, 2012. Several families are still trying to recover from the devastation and ruin which the storm left behind. Those who heeded the warning and escaped to the hurricane centers saved their lives though properties were lost and perished.

The Creator of heaven and earth has likewise in these last days extended invitation to you for the future event for pleasure and safety in eternity. Will you accept that invitation or will you ignore and spurn it? Today, says the Bible, is the acceptable day, (2 Corinthians 6:2; Acts of the Apostles 17:30). As you read this book, I pray for heaven's sunshine to illuminate your heart, awaken your spirit and soul, and prepare you a worthy pilgrim for God's New Jerusalem.

Reverend Samuel A. Abegunde

"He that is good for making excuses is seldom good for anything else." Benjamin Franklin

I HAVE PURCHASED A LAND

I HAVE A BUSINESS ENGAGEMENT

I HAVE FAMILY CARES

"For what is a man profited, if he shall gain the whole world, and lose his own soul? Or what shall a man give in exchange for his soul?" (Matt. 16:26 KJV).

Chapter One

I HAVE PURCHASED A LAND

But they all began, one after another, to make excuses. The first one told the servant, 'I have bought a field and must go and look at it; please accept my apologies.' Luke 14:18. (GNB).

It is a thing of joy to acquire land, build a house and own properties. But how would you acquire a land that you have not seen, checked out by some expert in the field and yourself? Would you not check to be sure you are not acquiring a swampy land, a garbage dump or a cemetery? Who does that? Men see fields before buying or paying for them and only purchase when they are sure and satisfied with what they see. Was the land seriously the object of an excuse here or he just used it as a silly, frivolous excuse to avoid the king's banquet? He ought to have seen the land before acquiring it. Going to see the piece of land in the evening, at supper time was improper and sounds ridiculously foolish. It could have been put off until the next morning during the daylight. The land will not run away or lose its value overnight. Would you like to make this kind of decision for yourself?

This is definitely the picture of a sinner who is materially minded. Of course, sinners will always feel that they are under certain necessities which make the duties of worship, reading of scriptures and prayers less important, disregarding the importance of attending to their souls' needs. Because of such pressing needs they lose every opportunity of grace; which God has extended to them. God has no regard for such excuses. Jesus rightly said, "What shall it profit a man if he shall gain the whole world but lose his own soul?" Mark 8:36-37. Jesus illustrated this with the story of the rich fool in Luke 12:16-21. The most important thing in life is not how much I am worth, but am I born again? Do I have a personal relationship with Jesus Christ?

Have your family responsibilities, especially children, become a reason which prevents you from the duties to worship and serve God? Have your work duties, doing overtime, now become your excuses, thereby forgetting there are many people out there that have no jobs. Someone was questioned by his Pastor why he failed to come to the house of worship? His reason was he was mowing his lawn on Sunday morning. Another time he was making or receiving telephone calls from a foreign country. Another person said he had financial needs, so he could not find any time right now to respond to the gospel. That is how many people turn the help, favor, and blessings received from God into obstructions and hindrances.

Giving excuses as a reason not to respond to the gospel invitation and serve God means four things:
1. You are dishonoring God
2. You are showing an attitude of indifference to your Maker
3. You are despising your Creator, and
4. You are playing a blame game, blaming God for his kindness. I would like you to read the

following scriptures to see what the Bible has to say about people who engage in these four things.

DISHONORING GOD

It is indeed a dishonor to reject the call of God upon your life. It is a dishonor to deprive God your presence and services. It is dishonoring when you spurn the face of the Almighty, when you think you can argue your way out of His power and glory.

INDIFFERENCE

You are at ease with contempt against God. You are careless by putting things of the earth at a higher priority against the things of the Spirit.

Psalm 123:4. *Our soul is exceedingly filled with the scorning of those that are at ease, and with the contempt of the proud.* (RV).

Isaiah 32:9. *Rise up, ye women that are at ease, and hear my voice; ye careless daughters, give ear unto my speech.* (RV).

Amos 6:1. *Woe to them that are at ease in Zion, and to them that are secure in the mountain of Samaria, the notable men of the chief of the nations, to whom the house of Israel come!* (RV).

Matthew 24:12. *And because iniquity shall be multiplied, the love of many shall wax cold.* (RV).

Matthew 22:5. *But they made light of it, and went their ways, one to his own farm, another to his merchandise:* (RV).

Isaiah 47:8. *Now therefore, hear this, thou that art given to pleasures, that dwellest carelessly, that sayest in thine heart, I am, and there is none else beside me; I shall not sit as a widow, neither shall I know the loss of children:* (RV).

DESPISE THE HOST
Proverbs 1:30. *They would none of my counsel; they despised all my reproof:*

Proverbs 9:8. *Reprove not a scorner, lest he hate thee: reprove a wise man, and he will love thee.*

Matthew 7:6. *Give not that which is holy unto the dogs, neither cast your pearls before the swine, lest haply they trample them under their feet, and turn and rend you.*

Acts 13:41. *Behold, ye despisers, and wonder, and perish; for I work a work in your days, a work which ye shall in no wise believe, if one declare it unto you.* (KJV)

2Peter 2:10. *But chiefly them that walk after the flesh in the lust of defilement, and despise dominion. Daring, self-willed, they tremble not to rail at dignities:* (KJV)

Romans 2:4. *Or despisest thou the riches of his goodness and forbearance and longsuffering, not knowing that the goodness of God leadeth thee to repentance* (RV).

IT IS PLAYING A BLAME GAME
The man using excuse in the evening for going to see a land which he has acquired was doing nothing more than playing a blame game. Don't forget that playing a blame game started from the

24

Garden of Eden when Adam blamed God for giving him Eve. Then Eve blamed the serpent. If God had to ask the serpent, I am almost sure the serpent would probably blame the devil and the blame game goes without end. In the past, I have confronted church members about why they were absent from the house of worship and I have received the following answers: "I was expecting a telephone call from Overseas", "It was my work duties", "The children did not wake up on time," "I have financial needs," etc. May God help them!

In spite of all these excuses, God is still saying, "come". There is still room today. You always have the opportunity today. His words declare to us in Acts 17:30, "The times of ignorance therefore God overlooked; but now he commandeth men that they should all everywhere repent:"

Acts 17:31. *In as much as he hath appointed a day, in the which he will judge the world in righteousness by the man whom he hath ordained; whereof he hath given assurance unto all men,*

*in that he hath raised him from the
dead.* (RV).

2 Corinthians 6:2. *For he saith, at an
acceptable time I hearkened unto thee,
And in a day of salvation did I succor
thee: behold, now is the acceptable
time; behold, now is the day of
salvation:* (ASV).

COME: It is the King's urgent invitation

Matthew 22:4. *Again he sent forth other
servants, saying, tell them that are
bidden, Behold, I have made ready my
dinner; my oxen and my fatlings are
killed, and all things are ready: come to
the marriage feast.*

COME: It is a gospel feast

Luke 14:17. *And he sent forth his
servant at supper time to say to them
that were bidden, come; for all things
are now ready.*

COME: It is a threefold call

Revelations 22:17. *And the Spirit and
the bride say, Come. And he that
heareth, let him say, Come. And he that*

is athirst, let him come: he that will, let him take the water of life freely.

COME: To the place of safety
Genesis 7:1. *And Jehovah said unto Noah, Come thou and all thy house into the ark; for thee have I seen righteous before me in this generation.*

COME: For the rest of your soul
Matthew 11:28. *Come unto me, all ye that labor and are heavy laden, and I will give you rest.*

COME: To a goodly fellowship
Numbers 10:29. *And Moses said unto Hobab, the son of Reuel the Midianite, Moses' father-in-law. We are journeying unto the place of which Jehovah said, I will give it you: come thou with us, and we will do thee good; for Jehovah hath spoken good concerning Israel.*

COME: For personal cleansing
Isaiah 1:18. *Come now, and let us reason together, saith Jehovah: though your sins be as scarlet, they shall be as white as snow; though they be red like crimson, they shall be as wool.*

COME: For a satisfying portion

Isaiah 55:1. *Ho, every one that thirsteth, come ye to the waters, and he that hath no money; come ye, buy, and eat; yea, come, buy wine and milk without money and without price.*

Chapter Two

I HAVE A BUSINESS ENGAGEMENT

> *Another one said, 'I have bought five pairs of oxen and am on my way to try them out; please accept my apologies.' Luke 14:19. (GNB).*

Buying machines and tools for business is a desirable, good thing. It is commendable and a sign of progress in our competitive world. However, this man in our discussion bought five yokes of Oxen without proving them. Who does that? No one buys five yokes of Oxen without first testing them; no one buys a car, a shoe, a suit, or a house without first proving it by way of seeing and testing it. Or couldn't he try them at any other time? This is just another flimsy excuse and a calculated insult to the host.

This shows this man as a man of considerable wealth who is trying to get ahead in the world, and there is nothing wrong in doing that. However, several people are like him who allow their business, occupation, career, and pursuit of material wealth to keep them away from God. There is nothing wrong with working and making money; after all, purchasing of property is the rich man's luxury. It is only when career or business or money-making prevents you from serving God or takes the place of God that it becomes sinful.

Someone once said that, "this life is a blip of time; its moments are filled with opportunities to do something significant". However, significance is not found in happiness, accumulation of wealth or any earthly possession. Significance could only be found in our relationship with God and people. It is only relationship that will survive death; anything you have done for the Kingdom will be remembered while everything else is lost. Those who acquired land, or married a wife, and this man who bought five yokes of Oxen, taxis, cars, or machines may be enjoying life (so to say); yet, those things become objects of distraction from God.

Pastor Alexander once told the story of a Nurse in his church. This lady's attendance in the church suddenly dropped. The Pastor and church members tried all their best to get her back to her faithfulness and commitments to Christ but they were unsuccessful. Then a fellow asked her the reason for staying away so long from the House of God? The lady replied that she was pursuing buying a new Mercedes SUV with cash, hence a lot of overtime hours, and as soon as this project was met she would come back to the church and her services would continue. Well, the lady bought the Mercedes SUV of her choice after some time. She had not used that SUV for a long time when she suddenly collapsed and became hospitalized.

While she was lying down critically ill, uncertain whether she would make it or not, one of her relations was driving the SUV both to visit her in the hospital and doing his own business. This shows the foolishness of thinking and planning without God. The Bible asks, "What do you have that was not given"? (1Corinthians 4:7). If what you have, including your very life is a gift from

God, then why will you not give your life
and services to that giver Who is God?

Chapter Three

I HAVE FAMILY ISSUES

Another one said, 'I have just gotten married, and for that reason I cannot come. Luke 14:20. (GNB).

It is a wonderfully good, great thing to be married, but when marriage becomes an object for excuses that takes away important function there may be a hidden motive or agenda. The marriage becomes an excuse, just blame it on your wife.

This man's excuse was, "I have just married a wife". Is this excuse not even sillier than the previous ones? Could he and his newly wedded wife not have been equally welcomed to the feast? Supper time was the chief of feasting time but because of this man's worldly gratification, marriage became a hindrance and reason for excuse. He valued temporary good at a higher price and at the expense of spiritual good. He esteemed temporal things higher than what heaven offers.

This man knew about his wedding when he initially accepted the invitation; and there was no reason why he could not attend the supper with his wife if he wished to do so. Are you afraid of what your family or friends will say or think of you should you accept Christ? In Christ's days, people gave excuses too (Luke 9:57-62). There will always be a reason for excuse. One thing is certain, though, no one who rejected this invitation had a good reason to do so. There will be no justifiable reason today as well for anyone to turn a deaf ear to the gospel of our Lord Jesus Christ and to invitation to accept Him as Lord and Savior.

Excuses can begin with, "I am tired, I am busy, or I am stressed" Or you blame it on your past, blame it on the devil, "the devil made me do it", "everybody knows I have problems with anger" or "I was abused as a child", and the excuses go without end. However, whatever our excuses are or may be, you will discover that excuses are frail, flimsy, lame, shallow, silly, and feeble. Will your excuses keep you away from God's party, His kingdom and His presence?

The three folks we read about in Luke 14:15-20 are a representation of many of us who offer various excuses as reasons not to attend to the things of God. The quest for money, happiness, pleasure, power, fame, position are behind all these excuses. True happiness, lasting pleasure, enjoyment, power, position and fame are not found in money, wealth and accumulation of worldly goods, else, Jay Gould, a famous American Millionaire, when he was dying would not have said, "I suppose I am the most miserable man on earth." Lord Beaconsfield, another man who enjoyed position and fame, wrote late in his life, "Youth is a mistake, manhood a s t r u g g l e ,   o l d   a g e   a regret." (WorldPress.com weblog)

What about Alexander the Great? He thought he would find pleasure in power, fame and military conquests. After Alexander had conquered the known world in his own time and having attained great military glory, history recorded that he went to his tent and wept. When he was asked why he wept he said, "Because there is no more world to conquer."

Take note that as a military commander, he was undefeated and the most successful throughout history. History recorded that as he was on his way home from conquering many countries, he came down with some illness. At that moment, his captured territories, powerful army, sharp swords, and wealth all had no meaning to him. He realized that death would soon arrive and he would be unable to return to his homeland. He told his officers: "I will soon leave this world. I have three final wishes. You need to carry out what I tell you." His generals, in tears, agreed. He said,

"My first wish is to have my physician bring my coffin home alone. My second wish is to scatter the gold, silver, and the gems from my treasure-house along the path to the tomb when you ship my coffin to the grave. My final wish is to put my hands outside the coffin." People surrounding him, the writer says, were very curious, but no one dared to ask the reason. However, his most favored general kissed his hand and asked; "my majesty, we will follow your instruction.

But can you tell us why you want us to do it this way?" Alexander said, "I want everyone to understand the three lessons I have learned. To let my physician carry the coffin alone is to let people realize that a physician cannot really cure people's illness. Especially when they face death, the physicians are powerless. I hope people will learn to treasure their lives. My second wish is to tell people not to be like me in pursuing wealth. I spent my whole life pursuing wealth, but I was wasting my time most of the time. My third wish is to let people understand that I came to this world with empty hands and I will leave this world also in empty hands." (PureInsight.org).

David, the King of Israel, loved women, and he had several of them. Later in his life the entire nation sought for and brought to him the most beautiful lady found in Israel, the most beautiful virgin, betrothed to no man. But the Bible record says that David could no longer engage in sexual activities despite his lifelong weakness for women (1Kings 1:1-5). This shows that whatever you are currently using as excuses which prevent your intimacy with God, your Creator, and with his Son, Jesus Christ, will one of these days become useless, unprofitable, and of no value to you.

The three individuals we have considered in Luke 14:15-20 had but silly, flimsy excuses. They valued temporal properties, career, and relations higher than things of eternity. Land, Oxen, and wife were more important than to be in the presence of God. Those are things that could wait; this banquet will happen only once in the history of this world, and there will never be any like it. Are you afraid of what family and friends will say if you show yourself as one who loves the Lord and dedicates yourself to his services? It is certain; no one who rejects this invitation has a good reason to do so. So also, there will be no justifiable reasons for anyone to turn a deaf ear to the gospel of our Lord Jesus Christ and to His invitation to the great supper of His Father.

Apostle Paul rightly said in Romans 1:20 that sin is inexcusable. In Genesis 3:12, Adam gave excuses for eating the forbidden fruit. In Exodus 32:24 Aaron offered excuses for making a golden calf. In 1Samuel 13:12, King Saul rendered excuses for usurping the functions of the Priest. King Saul again offered excuses for keeping the forbidden spoil in 1Samuel 15:21.

"He who excuses himself, accuses himself" Gabriel Meuriar

I AM NOT COMPETENT

I HAVE NO SOCIAL STANDING

I HAVE PERSONAL WEAKNESS

Moreover whom he did predestinate, them he also called: and whom he called, them he also justified: and whom he justified, them he also glorified. (Romans 8:30 KJV).

Chapter Four

I AM NOT COMPETENT

But Moses said to God, "I am nobody. How can I go to the king and bring the Israelites out of Egypt?" Exodus 3:11. (GNB)

But Moses said, "No, LORD, don't send me. I have never been a good speaker, and I haven't become one since you began to speak to me. I am a poor speaker, slow and hesitant." Exodus 4:10. (GNB)

Suppose you are God and you are looking for somebody to go and preach to human beings so that they will not be lost, who will you choose? Would you like to send -
1. A great military leader?
2. A skilled politician?
3. A musician?
4. An economist?
5. An administrator
6. A Moses?
7. An Angel?

Moses was an 80 year old man, fugitive from justice, wanted for murder in Egypt. He was educated but that was over 40 years ago. He was a prince in Egypt, popular and politically connected, but that was a long time ago and before he committed murder. It would not make any sense to send Moses; I probably would suggest ordaining some reputable angel to do the job the way it is supposed to be done. God chose to send Moses, and Moses, like some other servants, had reasons or excuses why he would not be the right candidate for the job. Moses gave God five excuses. We must be reminded that we also have received from God the calling to go to the world to preach deliverance to those in the bondage of sin, Mark 16:15 "And he said unto them, Go ye into all the world, and preach the gospel to the whole creation." (ASV)

FIRST EXCUSE: "Who am I?" Exodus 3:11
Moses was once a prince of Egypt; now he is a shepherd: an 80 year old man, passed average life span for his generation: a man wanted for murder in the very city where God wanted to send

him, hence his excuse for unwillingness to go. Moses gave the excuse of inability, he had no sword, no army to go to Pharaoh to demand the release of God's people. Whereas, Pharaoh who had a mighty army, could ask for Moses' head. Many in our churches wrestle with the thoughts of inability just like Moses; they give up before they start. Are you saying that God doesn't know what He is doing? God has the full knowledge of our weaknesses and inabilities; Psalm 139:1 - 18 has the following to say,

> *LORD, thou hast searched me, and*
> *   known me.*
> *2. Thou knowest my downsitting*
> *   and mine uprising, thou*
> *   understandest my thought afar*
> *   off.*
> *3. Thou searchest out my path and*
> *   my lying down, and art*
> *   acquainted with all my ways.*
> *4. For there is not a word in my*
> *   tongue, but, lo, O LORD, thou*
> *   knowest it altogether.*
> *5. Thou hast beset me behind and*
> *   before, and laid thine hand*
> *   upon me.*

6. *Such knowledge is too wonderful for me; it is high, I cannot attain unto it.*

7. *Whither shall I go from thy spirit? Or whither shall I flee from thy presence?*

8. *If I ascend up into heaven, thou art there: if I make my bed in Sheol, behold, thou art there.*

9. *If I take the wings of the morning, and dwell in the uttermost parts of the sea;*

10. *Even there shall thy hand lead me, and thy right hand shall hold me.*

11. *If I say, surely the darkness shall overwhelm me, and the light about me shall be night;*

12. *Even the darkness hideth not from thee, but the night shineth as the day: the darkness and the light are both alike to thee.*

13. *For thou hast possessed my reins: thou hast covered me in my mother's womb.*

14. *I will give thanks unto thee; for I am fearfully and wonderfully made: wonderful are thy works; and that my soul knoweth right well.*

15. *My frame was not hidden from thee, when I was made in secret, and curiously wrought in the lowest parts of the earth.*
16. *Thine eyes did see mine unperfect substance, and in thy book were all my members written, which day by day were fashioned, when as yet there was none of them.*
17. *How precious also are thy thoughts unto me, O God! How great is the sum of them!*
18. *If I should count them, they are more in number than the sand: when I awake, I am still with thee.* (RV)

GOD'S RESPONSE: Exodus 3:12
"I will certainly be with you", God promised to be with Moses. Paul said in Romans 8:31 "If God be for us, who can be against us?" Are some of us not making the same excuse today? It is true that we are not sufficient in and of ourselves, our sufficiency is in Christ according to 2Corinthians 3:5-6. God's presence will make a weak person to become strong, put honor on the worthless; God's presence will subdue

mountains, make difficulties melt like wax and, grant success to the unsuccessful. For example, see what Jesus used the uneducated fishermen to achieve in Acts of the Apostles 4:13. Just as God promised Moses of his presence in Exodus 3:12, so did Jesus give us assurance in Matthew 28:20.

SECOND EXCUSE: "WHAT IS HIS NAME?" Exodus 3:13.

Moses knew there would be a lot of questions from Israelites ranging from who is this God? Where are we going since we have been here for over 400 years? Moses felt inadequate, and ill prepared to answer these questions. Moses was saying, "I don't know enough about who you are and about your word". As we obey God and do His business, in every challenge, he shows himself anew to us. We must never allow lack of money, education or skill to stop us from what God wants us to do even when we cannot see the resources needed within or around us. Do not measure yourself against the task, measure God who is above every obstacle (Ephesians 3:20).

Talking of inadequacies, Daniel must have felt inadequate beside the lions, David before Goliath, the three Hebrews in the fiery furnace, and Noah beside the Ark. It is always a challenge to heed the call, but when you move by faith, you begin to feel the presence of God, which is greater and mightier than any obstacle.

I agree with Moses that it is a thing of high concern that those who speak to people in the name of God should be well prepared before they do. Matthew Henry's Bible Commentary says, "Those who would know what to say must go to God, to the word of his grace and to the throne of his grace, for instructions." Ezekiel 2:7; 3:4

GOD'S RESPONSE: Exodus 3:14-15
"Thus shall you say,"
God again instructed Moses what to say should the Israelites ask questions. Are we not like Moses today as we give similar excuses of our inadequacies? Jesus told us what to say in Mark 16:15-16; see also Paul's admonition, 1Corinthians 15:1-4; 2:2. Yet the man Moses raised his third excuse against God's call upon his life.

THIRD EXCUSE: "They will not believe me." Exodus 4:1.

Moses was then afraid of failure; he seemed to have forgotten that God said he would back him up. People will think Moses is lying, they will not believe him. Fear of failure suggests people will think I am crazy when I begin to talk about a personal relationship with Jesus. God assured Moses that there would be no doubt in the minds of the skeptics.

GOD'S RESPONSE:

As in the previous cases, God responded to Moses' excuse by showing him three convincing proofs. One, Moses's shepherd rod turned into a serpent, Exodus 4:2-5. Two, Moses's own hand became leprous, Exodus 4:6-8 and, three, water turned into blood when poured on dry ground, Exodus 4:9.

Like Moses, some of us hesitate to share the gospel of our Lord Jesus Christ because of fear of failure. Has Jesus not equally given us convincing proofs as done to Moses, according to both Romans 10:17 and John 20:30-31. In spite of those proofs, Moses proceeded yet to another excuse.

FOURTH EXCUSE: "I am slow of speech and slow of tongue" Exodus 4:10
Moses gave another excuse that he was not an eloquent speaker forgetting that God is not moved by eloquent speeches. God knows the inabilities and disabilities of those He chooses to run an errand for Him, Exodus 4:11. God arranged for Aaron to be Moses' mouthpiece – Aaron was the greatest mistake that Moses allowed in his life. Aaron was the reason why Miriam became sick with leprosy. Aaron was behind the making of a golden calf when Moses was away, which inadvertently led to the death of thousands of Israelites.

As a Pastor for over forty years, I can attest to having known individuals who overcome impediments of speech such as stammering and become excellent preachers and teachers of the word without a trace of imperfect speech.
Like Moses, people have used infirmity as excuse to evade the call of God. Excuses include education, physical

49

handicap, age, income, distance etc. These are not legitimate excuses for not serving the Lord. God was well aware of it before choosing you for His work.

Jesus has given us a helper in the person of the Holy Spirit. The work of the Holy Spirit is unlike the works of Aaron, who led people to sin. Our helper, the Holy Spirit will live within us and teach us all things (John 16:15). Should your excuse be that of some infirmity like Moses, be reminded that God spoke through Balaam's ass, used a rooster to speak to Peter, and used an old sheep hide to speak to Gideon. He can as well use you if you are available for him.

FIFTH EXCUSE: "SEND WHOMEVER ELSE YOU MAY SEND" Exodus 13
This is the real reason for all the excuses. Moses did not want to go, and he had no interest in the assignment of God. Did Jonah want to go to Nineveh? Of course not. All the previous excuses which Moses gave were to hide the real fact. Then God's anger was kindled against Moses, Exodus 4:14a. Also, read verses 15-17 where there is a strong emphasis on the word "shall" to see the

anger of God. The anger of the Lord is against those who do not live up to their calling. We know the rest of the story; Moses answered that call and went to Egypt, and the children of Israel were delivered. What about us? What will the rest of our story be? Are you making excuses not to respond to God's call? What are you waiting for? May God give you the grace to go.

Chapter Five

LACK OF SOCIAL STANDING

Judges 6:11-16. *And the angel of the LORD came and sat under the oak which was in Ophrah, that pertained unto Joash the Abiezrite: and his son Gideon was beating out wheat in the winepress, to hide it from the Midianites.*

12. *And the angel of the LORD appeared unto him, and said unto him, The LORD is with thee, thou mighty man of valour.*

13. *And Gideon said unto him, Oh my lord, if the LORD be with us, why then is all this befallen us? And where be all his wondrous works which our fathers told us of, saying, Did not the LORD bring us up from Egypt? But now the LORD hath cast us off, and delivered us into the hand of Midian.*

14. *And the LORD looked upon him, and said, Go in this thy might, and save Israel from the hand of Midian: have not I sent thee?*

15. And he said unto him, Oh Lord, wherewith shall I save Israel? Behold, my family is the poorest in Manasseh, and I am the least in my father's house.
16. And the LORD said unto him, surely I will be with thee, and thou shalt smite   the Midianites as one man. (GNB).

BACKGROUND TO GIDEON'S CALL

It is a known fact that Israel was prone to forgetting God, neglecting his services, worshipping idols and living a life of unfaithfulness in her times of prosperity; the time which they were made comfortable and peaceful in their homes and businesses. At such times, God, in turn, sends them enemy nations who then afflict, and terrorize them as in the current case (Judges 6:2-6). They were reduced to living in caves, mountain dens and strongholds. Their farm products destroyed, sheep, ox, cattle, asses taken away from them, left bitter and impoverished (Chapter 6:6). These were the reasons why they started calling on God for deliverance.

To cry to God only during trouble, hardship, adversity, tragedy and calamity is a sign of selfishness and ingratitude. That seems to be the only language to soften their hearts; and open their ears to make them turn back to God.

RELIEF NOT IMMEDIATE
It is good to recognize God and call upon him to deliver us from enemies; we should remember that relief may not always be immediate, especially when the problem was caused by our previous neglect of God. They cried unto God in the current situation, and God did not send them a deliverer right away, instead, he sent a Prophet (chapter 6:7-10). The Prophet did not predict immediate relief, did not give any revelation or inspiration. Like previous Prophets, he showed them their character, recounted the past goodness and mercy of God, then charged them with the sin of ingratitude and apostasy. Through the Prophet, God dealt with their sins because He wanted to heal their sins before physical deliverance. God is not in a hurry to deliver; He does not run out of time.

I have observed that all the people the Lord called were called while actively on duty, some their own personal business, others working for their family and others on other people's business. Examples are Gideon, Moses, Samuel, Amos, Paul, and Peter, to name a few. God never called an idle or a lazy person to be his Prophet, Priest, Judge, or a deliverer.

I have also observed from my study of the scriptures that the Lord uses various methods to call his servants; Peter was called while fishing. Paul was called while he was going to persecute Christians, as he saw a vision of Him. God called Samuel in the tabernacle. He showed Moses a burning bush. Isaiah saw the vision of Him in the Temple.

Now, the children of Israel, the Bible says in Judges 6:1-3 that they did evil in the sight of the Lord by not following the law God gave to them and by serving the god of the Amorites. Because of this disobedience, God allowed the Midianites to terrorize them for seven years. They will plant in their farms, but the enemies will come and reap the harvest. The Israelites became powerless and greatly impoverished by the Midianites (Judges 6:6). This happened for a period of seven years.

Sad to say that the situation of the Israelites mentioned here is similar to the lives of many people in our world today. People disregard the laws of God, and will not give to God their worship. They don't care about God as long as things are going well with them, as long as they have jobs and are not sick. God had to use the Midianites, Amalekites and the children of the East (v. 3) as a whip to turn their hearts and attention back to himself. Does God need to do that to you in order for you to turn your attention and heart to your creator? Ecclesiastes chapter 12:1-3 says to us,

1. *Remember also thy Creator in the days of thy youth, or ever the evil days come, and the years draw nigh, when thou shalt say, I have no pleasure in them;*
2. *Or ever the sun, and the light, and the moon, and the stars,*

*be darkened, and the clouds
return after the rain:
3. in the day when the keepers of
the house shall tremble, and the
strong men shall bow
themselves, and the grinders
cease because they are few, and
those that look out of the
windows be darkened,*

Chapter 6:7 says, "They cried unto the Lord." In answer to their cry the LORD Himself chose to visit them.

Judges 6:11-12. And the angel of the LORD came and sat under the oak which was in Ophrah, that pertained unto Joash the Abiezrite: and his son Gideon was beating out wheat in the winepress, to hide it from the Midianites.
12. And the angel of the LORD appeared unto him, and said unto him, The LORD is with thee, thou mighty man of valour.

I would not want to miss important information about the appearance of the "Angel of the LORD" mentioned in verses 11 and 12. There are several appearances of the Angel of the LORD in both the Old and New Testaments. These are the appearances I will refer to as "Theophany." It means the appearance of God to man in physical form. We can also call it "Christophany." They were the occasions when Christ appeared to individuals. Here is a list of some of them.

The Angel of the LORD appeared to Hagar in Genesis 16.
The Angel of the LORD appeared to Abram in Genesis 22
The Angel of the LORD appeared to Moses in Exodus 3:1-6
The Angel of the LORD appeared to Balaam in Numbers 22
The Angel of the LORD appeared to all the people in Judges 2:1
The Angel of the LORD appeared to Manoah and his wife in Judges 13
The Angel of the LORD visited Israel in 2Samuel 24
The Angel of the LORD appeared to Gideon in Judges 6:12.

We can conclude from the above appearances in the Old Testament that the Angel of the LORD is none other than Christ Himself, God the Son, who appeared in the form of an Angel, a man or fire holding conversations with man.

GIDEON'S RESPONSE TO THE ANGEL

Please bear in mind that at this time Gideon was not aware of the identity of the man who was trying to get into conversation with him. I am sure that the Angel must have got Gideon irritated by his greeting when the Angel said, "The LORD is with thee, thou mighty man of valour (Judges 6:12). Gideon reacted with questions in verse 13 this way, "And Gideon said unto him, Oh my lord, if the LORD be with us, why then is all this befallen us? And where be all his wondrous works which our fathers told us of, saying, Did not the LORD bring us up from Egypt? But now the LORD hath cast us off, and delivered us into the hand of Midian." (RV)

Gideon was asking, "If the LORD be with us why is our situation like this?" He also questioned the story of past miracles and the dealing of God with His people Israel. He must have been thinking on the stories he had heard about God, trying to make sense of the meaning of his country's situation, "If God be with a man ought he not to prosper?" He was right to observe that God was not present with them; however, he was wrong in not seeing why God turned away from them. Are you asking questions too like Gideon? Why is your situation in life like the way it is? Gideon was asking the right questions but he did not take time to look at his own father's house and all Israel. If he did, he would have found reasons why God abandoned them. For example, Gideon's father was a Baal worshiper; the rest of Israel went the same way worshipping foreign gods, which God had warned them against. How come Gideon could not trace their problems to their disobedience? Like Gideon, it is often easy for us to see what God has not done for us or in our lives, while we are often blind to our responsibilities to God, which we have failed to give to him.

In response, the Angel of the LORD addressed Gideon as; "Mighty Warrior." Gideon did not see himself as a mighty warrior; rather, he saw himself as the least in his family and saw his tribe as insignificant or unpopular in Israel. I think he was right to have seen himself that way because he had no previous military training or battle experience to qualify him for that title. He had no religious or political affiliation. I think he was at that stage a skeptic taken from idol worshipping, like Abraham. He came when the situation was at its worst. Moreover, he was hiding where he was at the time, so how can you call him a mighty warrior? One of the important points which we must glean here is the fact that God does not see you the way you see and evaluate yourself. God sees you and what you can accomplish when you are in Him. This is why Simon, who denied Jesus, could become Peter the Rock, Abraham, the father of no children, could become the father of multitudes.

Second, like Gideon, when you look at yourself, you'll probably see past mistakes, failures, inadequacies but when the LORD looks at you, He sees something totally different. God saw a king in David when Jesse did not regard him important to be a son (1Samuel 16:12). He saw a warrior in Gideon when he was hiding from the Midianites. God is able to take us and transform us to what he wants us to be.

My third point is that we all react differently to life's problems, obstacles and challenges. For example, there was an episode during which Jesus asked his disciples to give the multitudes something to eat (Matt 14:14-16). The disciples looked at their resources and the numbers of the crowd they were to feed; they quickly concluded that five loaves and two fishes were insufficient. Jesus took the same loaves and fishes, gave thanks and the people were fed with food left over. Sometimes we are like Gideon and the disciples of Christ, faced with life's problems, difficulties and, obstacles. I pray that we will be encouraged not to meet those moments or seasons with fear or hiding, but with courage and determination. As we look at our own circumstances and our seemingly limited resources, may we not conclude like Gideon and the disciples of Jesus that we are hopeless and helpless.

Though the Midianites did not know where Gideon was hiding, the LORD knew it and went straight to him.

Likewise, the LORD knows us, knows where we are and our situation, through every valley and every mountain (Hebrews 13:5, Matthew 28:20). His words made us to know that He knows you better than you know yourself (Psalm 139; Hebrews 4:13).

Another point demonstrated here is that God often uses unlikely instruments or persons to achieve his goals and purposes (1Corinthians 1:26-29). This point is clearly demonstrated in the case of Gideon in Judges 6:7. Here are several other examples of unlikely or insignificant instruments which God uses: the shepherd's rod of Moses in Exodus 4:2, jaw bone of a donkey in Judges 15:15, David's five smooth stones (1Samuel 17:40), handful of meal and a cruise of oil (1King 17:12), a cloud the size of a man's hand in 1Kings 18:44, the mustard seed (Matthew 13:32) and five barley loaves (John 6:9).

God used Abraham, a man from a pagan family from Ur of the Chaldees;
God used Jacob, a supplanter, to become the father of Israel;

God used Joseph, a slave boy, to save the entire world from hunger;
God used Moses, a murderer and fugitive, to deliver the nation of Israel;
God used Jephtah, the son of a prostitute, to deliver Israel;
God used a slave girl to obtain healing for Naaman and to tell him about God;
God used Saul of Tarsus, the persecutor to write several Epistles in the New Testament;
God used Matthew a tax collector to write about Jesus the King of the Jews.

You think God cannot use you? Maybe He is calling you right now. Can you hear him? Calling you to go out to the streets, high ways and by-ways, with the gospel to evangelize the unreached. Maybe he is calling you to teach or sing, visit the homeless, go to the shelters, prisons, and clothe the naked. May you hear Him today?

Outward appearance, family history, rank, and social class mean nothing to God; they are not the criteria God uses to find the right person to do his job. The one he uses may be in the fishing boat, by the sheep fold or on the threshing floor. He calls; people change their course and destiny because He sends them with His presence.

THE PHURAH FACTOR

Judges 7:10. "But if thou fear to go down, go thou with Phurah thy servant down to the camp:" This instruction from God illustrates two points in this story. One, when God calls you he will also call some other individuals to go with you. Those individuals could be members of your own family or outside of your family, who will give you support and encouragement when the going gets tough. Plus, God's own presence also goes with you. At no time will you be alone in your calling except for testing.

The second illustration deals with times when obstacles or doubts are put in your way, and you need a strong, dependable support. For example, initially Gideon's Army was 32,000 men strong; all of a sudden, God reduced that number to 300 to face huge trained Forces of three countries with sophisticated weaponry, whereas, Gideon's Army had no equipment to match that of the enemy. I believe that situation calls for fear and doubt. Fear and doubts are real when you are working for God. That is why you need individuals of like mind and thirst for God to journey with you. I thank God for the wife He graciously gave me. She has remained steady and un-shaken through all my tough times in the ministry when those who started with me suddenly quit in the middle of the road. It is sad, though, that some men of God thought they could do the work of God alone. I am sure that no matter how powerful a man or woman of God may be, he or she needs others in order to fulfill the calling.

A WORD OF CAUTION TO LEADERS
There are about six lessons we should not miss as we talk about the call of Gideon. These lessons are about the conduct or attitude of the individuals that we are leading. Every leader needs to be aware and watch for these actions in the life of people that they lead which may manifest themselves any time along the journey to heaven. These conducts or attitudes will make a man or woman unfit for doing anything noteworthy for God.

1. **Fear and cowardice**: (Judges chapter 7:3) Notice that 32,000 soldiers gathered around Gideon

and God said that anyone that is afraid should return; 22,000 returned instantly. Cowards are always untrustworthy, you cannot rely on cowards, they will not fight, and they will become a burden and hindrance. God said, let them return because you are better off without them. Don't let numbers fool you. Remember Israel's cowardice before Goliath, 1Samuel 17:24; David before Absalom, 2Samuel 15:14; Ephraim, Psalm 78:9; The Disciples of Jesus in Matthew 26:56.

2. **Those who bowed to drink** (Judges Chapter 7:5-6). Weak soldiers, divided of heart who bowed their knees, not firm, could not be in haste. Too relaxed in a war front is an attitude that does not belong to a soldier ready for a fight. God said, "return", 7,000 went back as well.

3. **Conduct of Ephraim:** (Judges Chapter 8:1) The tribe of Ephraim came complaining, angry and filled with confrontation, indignation, blame and sharp

contention that they were not consulted initially to be part of the overthrow. They wished they were part of the glory. By this behavior they were trying to show that if they were contacted initially, they would have gladly joined the fighting force. Persons of this mind set exist in our churches; they feel hurt that they were not consulted when a particular work or project or problems were being solved though they were there during the infancy of the problem. Leaders of Ephraim failed to recognize that not every job is a visible leadership role. Engineers and millionaires may design and finance a project; but it will take bricklayers, carpenters, electricians; painters and cleaners to get the job done. Pride is the only reason that makes us to seek recognition. They were jealous of what Gideon and his men were accomplishing. Jealousy is a disease; remember the jealousy of Joseph's brothers in Genesis 37:4; King Saul in

1Samuel 18:8; the older brother of the prodigal son in Luke 15:28 and the laborers in the vine yard in Matthew 20:12.

4. **The conduct of the leaders of Succoth** (Judges Chapter 8:5-6). The leaders and men of Succoth were blind, poor-spirited and selfish to the good of a common cause. They shut themselves up in their secured homes (fortified) and let Gideon's army starve. They refused to support God's appointed army. It was okay for them to see the work of God stop uncompleted. They had more than enough bread to satisfy their own hunger. These leaders were fearful with doubts that Gideon's army may not be able to subdue 1500 men since they were only 300 strong. Fear made them fail not to recognize God in their mission. With or without us, God will prevail, and then we would have missed God's victory and then face bitter consequences. Let us join our forces with those whom God has chosen to lead doing this work.

5. **The conduct of Penuel** (Judges Chapter 8:9). Copycat syndrome. Because the leaders of Succoth turned Gideon and his army away, the leaders of Penuel also decided to turn them away. It is a people who lack spiritual illumination, blind to a common good, and who do not have their own spine but will copy another. The word of God tells us not to follow multitudes to do evil (Exodus 23:2), Penuel just did that. They do not care if Israel remains subjected to Midian forever or if the work of God stopped uncompleted.

6. **The Conduct of Abimelech:** Abimelech was the 71st son of Gideon. He murdered 69 of his brothers in order to become king. He destroyed the good work, which his father had done over 40 years.

Chapter Six

Before I formed thee in the belly I knew thee, and before thou camest forth out of the womb I sanctified thee; I have appointed thee a prophet unto the nations. Jeremiah 1:5. (RV).

I answered, "Sovereign LORD, I don't know how to speak; I am too young." Jeremiah 1:6. (GNB).

There is a total of sixteen prophetic books in the Bible. These books are divided into major and minor prophets. The division is based not on importance or authenticity but on the length of the book. Jeremiah's Hebrew name means, "The Lord is exalted." He comes from Anathoth, a village few miles north of Jerusalem. Men from his tribe including his father and grandfather, were respected priests, so as he grew it would be normal for Jeremiah also to have been nursing the ambition that one day he would become a priest. I can imagine the strong opposition he would have faced when he told his dad and grandfather the first time that he was going to be a prophet. I can imagine his father saying nobody has ever been a prophet in this family.

JEREMIAH'S CALL Jeremiah 1:5
What was God saying in this verse? God was telling the young man that I know you longer than your parents. I knew you before I ordered your mother to conceive you, I have already planned your life, there is a purpose for your life. Let go of your own plans, though men from your tribe are respected Priests and Temple workers. I have a pre-existing work for you to be a Prophet to the nations. You are already ORDAINED, SANCTIFIED. That is what I think I hear God saying to him. But I am curious to know why God was dealing so gently with him. I believe God took this easy approach of speaking tenderly with him because of his age; he was a young man.

JEREMIAH'S EXCUSE Jeremiah 1:6
Jeremiah said, "I cannot speak. I am a child." Some scholars believe that Jeremiah was at that time between 16

and 20 years old, other scholars argued that he must have been between 20 and 25 years old. Whatever the school of thought you have come from, everyone believes that Jeremiah at that time was a youth under thirty years of age. So, when he said, "I cannot speak, I am a child", what was he talking about? To be a child could mean many things, immature, inexperienced, unmarried, and inferior among many other meanings.

We can always find an excuse not to obey God's call; Moses did the same in Exodus 4:10 and so many prophets gave excuses why they do not want to yield to God's call or run His errand, and Jonah is a good example of that. Some of our excuses among many are, "I am busy, I am not ready and I am poor, I am too young for that I want to enjoy my life first, I will do it some other time."

Like Jeremiah we often forget that with God age presents no barrier for him to use anyone he chooses to use. God used little Samuel who had no lesson on Theology to convey his message and intent to Eli the Priest, God used

Balaam's ass to warn Balaam who was in peril of wealth against God's directives, God used cockcrow to speak to Peter when he needed to remember his words, Jesus told the Jews that God could raise stones to praise God so that the religious Jews could understand that God can use anything he chooses to do his will and bring his message to anyone he wanted to communicate with.

Don't we often forget that when God calls you and me, it isn't because we earned it, it isn't because our application portfolio is the best and perfect, not because we are bright and eloquent or we are the best, not because we are the strongest and unbeatable; it is simply His choice, and he does not want anybody else to do it but the person which he has called to do the job.

DIFFERENCES BETWEEN PRIESTS AND PROPHETS

To be a prophet was a tough and demanding job for several reasons. The prophetic office was different from the priest's office for the following reasons. Prophets carry unpopular messages to those who do not want to hear them;

therefore, prophets are always in danger of being killed or imprisoned, but the priest is not always in danger. Priests' duties are predictable, written in the laws, but prophets will not know from one day where they will go the next day or what message they will be instructed by God to deliver. Priests work to preserve the past while prophets address the present so that the nation or individuals will amend their ways in order to have the future. Priests deal with sacrifices, rituals, offerings which are externals, whereas prophets deal with conducts and the hearts. Priests belong to a special tribe, but prophets could come from any tribe. The priests' offices command respect and authority and, they are supported from proceeds from offerings and sacrifices but the prophet must prove divine call and has no guaranteed income.

Note that Jesus traveled from coast to coast like the prophets, speaking to hearts, changing them so that they can have a future in heaven. Just as the prophets were despised, maltreated and their messages rejected and, in some cases, killed, so was Jesus treated.

GOD'S RESPONSE Jeremiah 1:7-9

> 7. *But the LORD said unto me,*
> *Say not, I am a child: for to*
> *whomsoever I shall send thee*
> *thou shalt go, and*
> *whatsoever I shall command*
> *thee thou shalt speak.*
> 8. *Be not afraid because of them:*
> *for I am with thee to deliver*
> *thee, saith the LORD.*
> 9. *Then the LORD put forth his*
> *hand, and touched my mouth;*
> *and the LORD said unto me,*
> *Behold, I have put my words in*
> *thy mouth:* (RV).

Three significant messages stand clear from the Lord's instruction above to Jeremiah. One, the rebuke in verse 7, which says, "Do not say that I am a child." Two, "I will be with you," in verse 8. Three, "The touching of his mouth," verse 9. It should be clear to every one of us that there is no one too young, too old, too rich, too poor, too busy or too anything for God to use and this fact has been demonstrated over and again in the scripture. When Abraham was 99 years old God called him and asked him to walk before him and be perfect (Genesis 17: 2). God called Samuel at about age 17. God called Moses at age 80 even though he had a bad record, and at a time when shepherds were not looked upon kindly because of their smelling environments. God can use, and will use anyone. This is a strong message that God sent to Jeremiah in verse 7.

In verse 8, God gave Jeremiah the message of promise, "I will be with you." That is the message of God's presence. This means if God sent you, then you are not alone; you have a formidable traveling companion. We must understand, as Jeremiah did, that before we can really enjoy the presence of God and see Him in action, we have to go to where he sends us, speak what God wants us to say and reject fear. Then, as you go, God begins to reveal Himself more and more. I can tell you with every certainty that each problem you encounter will bring you a new experience of God. For example, some of the children of Israel did not know God as the God who could deliver from the hands of Pharaoh until it happened and they left Egypt. Others did not know him as the God who could feed the hungry even in the wilderness until God rained down manna and provided water out of the rock. There are those servants of God even today who are not convinced that they do not need to lie and cheat before God can meet their daily needs, and my heart goes out to them.

The third message is the touching of Jeremiah's mouth by God in verse 9. The touch of God does so many things in our lives. Specifically, for Jeremiah, it purified and inspired him. This reminds me of a hymn by Allan McGee which we used to sing, it is titled, "He Touched Me."

Looking at the ministry of our Lord Jesus will show us His work in the lives of people He touched and what His touch can do and achieve in all of our lives too. The touch of Christ is a:
Cleansing touch Matthew 8:3. And he stretched forth his hand, and touched him, saying, I will; be thou made clean. And straightway his leprosy was cleansed.

Quieting touch Matthew 8:15. And he touched her hand, and the fever left her; and she arose, and ministered unto him.

Illuminating touch Matthew 9:29. Then touched he their eyes, saying, according to your faith be it done unto you.

Matthew 9:30. And their eyes were opened. And Jesus strictly charged them, saying, See that no man know it.

Liberating touch Mark 7:33. And he took him aside from the multitude privately, and put his fingers into his ears, and he spat, and touched his tongue;

Mark 7:34. and looking up to heaven, he sighed, and saith unto him, Ephphatha, that is, Be opened.

Mark 7:35. And his ears were opened, and the bond of his tongue was loosed, and he spake plain.

Blessing touch Mark 10:13. And they brought unto him little children, that he should touch them: and the disciples rebuked them.

Mark 10:14. But when Jesus saw it, he was moved with indignation, and said unto them, suffer the little children to come unto me; forbid them not: for of such is the kingdom of God.

Mark 10:15. Verily I say unto you, whosoever shall not receive the kingdom of God as a little child, he shall in no wise enter therein.

Mark 10:16. And he took them in his arms, and blessed them, laying his hands upon them.

Healing touch Luke 22:51. But Jesus answered and said, Suffer ye thus far. And he touched his ear, and healed him.

THE MESSAGE (Jeremiah 1:10)
Jeremiah would soon find out that his assignment was costly and challenging. His message would not bring him fame and adoration; instead, it would leave him in prison, make him more enemies than friends. Little wonder he preached for 40 years without a single convert. If you were to grade Jeremiah how would you rate him? Pass or fail?

Prophet Jeremiah spoke against injustice, oppression, corruption, immorality, against sin and punishment. He was arrested, imprisoned, taken captive and sent to exile. When he returned, he continued to proclaim the message of God.

Perhaps, God is calling you right now to make a difference somewhere. Perhaps, He is asking you to serve your community in some special way. Maybe, He is calling you to serve in a particular department in your church, or to fund a project. Perhaps, God wants you to speak out wherever injustice rules or where violence prevails over peace. Maybe, he is calling you to be a friend to someone hurting right now. Maybe, he is calling you to write a petition or stage a demonstration. Can you hear him? Are you listening?

I read that in the glory days of the Roman Empire, there was a time of state games in the Coliseum during which human beings battled with wild beasts or one another until one or both were dead. The crowd, I read, found pleasure and delight in the brutal death of a human being until one day in A.D. 404 when a Syrian monk by the name of Telemachus leaped to the Coliseum floor, because he was torn by a disregard for the value of a human being. The monk cried out, "In the name of God, this thing is not right, in the name of God, this thing must stop." Enraged spectators mocked the monk, some furiously threw objects at him, and the gladiators attacked him with a sword which pierced him. The monk fell to the ground dead. For the first time, the Coliseum fell silent because the people recognized the horror of what they had regarded as entertainment. Because of this courageous single act, the gladiatorial combat closed within months. One man dared to speak on behalf of God – many lives were saved. Telemachus died but his message prevailed.

"Whereas ye know not what shall be on tomorrow. For what is your life? It is even a vapour, that appeareth for a little time, and then vanisheth away."

James 4:14 KJV.

I WILL FOLLOW THEE

SUFFER ME FIRST TO BURY MY FATHER

WHY WE SHOULD GO TO CHURCH

For the gifts and calling of God are without repentance. (Romans 11:29 KJV).

Chapter Seven

MASTER, I WILL FOLLOW THEE

*"And there came a scribe,
and said unto him, Master,
I will follow thee
whithersoever thou goest.
And Jesus saith unto him,
the foxes have holes, and
the birds of the heaven
have nests; but the Son of
man hath not where to lay
his head." (Matthew 8:
19-20)*

To be a disciple of Jesus is a sacrifice that could be very costly; although, those outside of that circle may think it is easy and comfortable. Jesus did not have a place of his own called home. He had no bed to sleep on at night, no pillow to make his head comfortable, and no leisure time. He held no title to a car or landed property. He had no bank account. Jesus had no suitcase in which to pack his suits, changing attire, tooth brush and a towel. He wore sandals on the hot sands of Palestine deserts. So, to be a disciple of Jesus Christ will cost you all of this and more. To be a follower or disciple of Christ may cost you your habits, friends, your favorite lifestyles, but at the end you will discover it was an investment, which lasts for eternity and yields incredible rewards.

This un-named scribe came to Jesus un-invited and said, "Master, I will follow thee whithersoever thou goest." Matthew 8:19. Ordinarily, one would conclude that this scribe was different from the rest of the sect; he would have been classified as having good, honest and earnest desire to be a disciple of Christ. However, Christ response to his request that, "foxes have holes, and the birds of the heaven *have* nests; but the Son of man hath not where to lay his head," Luke 9: 58, suggests his motive. Christ, who knew the heart of every man he created, responded negatively to a hidden motive of a would-be disciple. He did not wait for his turn to be called like Christ called Peter, James, John and the rest. In Hebrews 5:4 it is written, "And no man taketh this honour unto himself, but he that is called of God, as was with Aaron."

The impulsive scribe who wanted to be a disciple has seen miracles. He has seen fame, the crowd of people as they meet the disciples everywhere with enthusiasm and excitement, and he was carried away with emotions and made a hasty decision to join without being called by Christ. The Savior's answer to him revealed his real motive, the much hidden part of the heart; he coveted the popularity, excitement and thrill that goes with being a disciple, which the disciples enjoyed while he failed to count the cost of being a pilgrim, sojourner and a stranger.

There are ministers and church ministries in our society today, who are not thinking differently from this scribe. Their quests are for spectacular excitement of the crowd and such mind set has become an acceptable norm. The thrill, the hype, the buzz, and the seeming success of events become a driving and motivating goal, be it right or wrong. These are those who believe in mega, attractive modern time methods as long as it appeals to their emotions and carries the badge "Christian". To them, it doesn't matter who you link with as long as it looks good from outward appearance; it does not matter what it looks like within. One of the dangers of being emotionally attached with a mega crowd and its excitement is that believers will not realize when they begin to drift still relying on emotional events, crowd and thrill rather than the Lord. When there is no more excitement here, they move somewhere else.

Perhaps, this scribe, having seen the miracles, fame and excitement that met Jesus and his disciples, thought that Jesus might one day become the long expected Messiah, then those around him would have the first advantage of ease, honor and wealth; thus, he offered himself. Disappointedly, Jesus declared the reality of what it meant to follow him, which is a denial of worldly temporary comfort. It is sad to note that we never heard of this man again in the rest of the Bible.

THE SCRIBES
Since we have been discussing this un-named scribe in this narrative, I think it will be in order to talk more about this sect in the Bible. This sect called scribes

were experts in legal matters; they were also religious teachers of the law. There were three notable things about their attitude towards Christ. One, they often accuse Christ of blasphemy, Mark 2:6-7. Two, they always question the Lord's authority for doing what he did in the life of people, be it a miracle, teaching or healing, Luke 20:1-2. Three, they always look for a way, chance or opportunity to accuse him of anything at all, Luke 6:7.

However, the Lord has a way he exposes them, Matthew 23:13-36. He condemns their behavior, Luke 20:46-47; he calls them hypocrites, Matthew 15:1-9. The characteristics of the scribes in the New Testament include showing external righteousness, Matthew 5:20 and teaching without authority, Matthew 7:29. The Scribes were collectors of Temple revenue, 2Kings 12:10; teachers of religious law, Ezra 7:6, 10, 12. They were advisers in State affairs, 1Chronicles 27:32. They were keepers of records, Jeremiah 36:25-26.

Chapter Eight

SUFFER ME FIRST TO BURY MY FATHER

"And another of the disciples said unto him, Lord, suffer me first to go and bury my father.
But Jesus saith unto him, Follow me; and leave the dead to bury their own dead." (Matthew 8: 21-22)

Ordinarily, this seemed to be a reasonable request and responsible respect for one's parents. However, was his father still alive or dead? Was he sick and at the point of death, or was he old and this disciple wanted to wait on him till death? These and other questions remain the subject of inquiry and arguments for scholars and theologians. We may never find an answer to those questions since the Evangelist who recorded the narrative did not follow up to give us the rest of the story. However, we know without a doubt that Christ, before whom this disciple stood, knows deep into the heart of this disciple and He answered him accordingly. It is evident that this disciple was conscious of the call, knew the need for it, but was asking for a delay using burying his father as an excuse. He was not objecting to his call or refusing it, or doubting this call. He was simply asking to be excused for a time so that he could bury his dad. We should know that he was not asking for permission to attend his dead father's funeral; instead, he wanted to put off following Jesus until his father died.

He was probably the first born son and wanted to claim his inheritance. Perhaps, he wanted to prevent his father's anger should he leave the family business to follow this free-lance preacher called Jesus. His immediate concern may have even been financial security, or probably he wanted to wait for his family's approval or something else. One thing that is sure is the fact that this disciple did not want to commit himself to Jesus right away. However, Jesus would not accept his excuse.

Jesus is always direct with those He calls or chooses to follow him, no diplomacy, no ifs, and no buts. They must count the cost and set aside the conditions they might have for following him. That is why he did not hesitate to place his demand of complete loyalty on the disciple. He made it clear to him and to all who follow him that family loyalty was not to take priority over the demands of obedience to God. His direct challenge forces us to ask ourselves about our priorities in following him. The decision to follow Jesus should not be put off, even though other loyalties compete for our attention. Nothing should be placed above a total commitment to living for him.

> *It is written, "He who laid his hands upon the plough and look back is not fit for the kingdom of God," (Luke 9:62).*

Jesus summoned him to an immediate decision, "Let the dead bury their dead." Matthew 8:22. Permit me to say that this disciple has no zeal for the work of Christ. He wanted to keep Christ in suspense; an unwilling mind will find an excuse for whatever he or she does not want to do. Christ once again here disallowed excuse; his excuse was shallow and insufficient.

NAZARITES:

Under the Mosaic laws, Nazarites were not allowed to mourn for their parents because they were holy unto the Lord, (Numbers 6:6-8). And the High Priest must not defile himself, not for his own father's death, (Leviticus 21:11-12). Christ, therefore, requires of those who will follow him that they hate their father and mother (Luke 14:26). This means, love father and mother less than you love God. Our relations cannot be in competition with God.

Chapter Nine

WHEN GOD INTERRUPTS OUR "I's" AND "MY's" SYNDROME

Please read Luke 12:16-21.

16. And he told them a parable, saying, "The land of a rich man produced plentifully,

17. And he thought to himself, 'What shall I do, for I have nowhere to store my crops?'

18. And he said, 'I will do this: I will tear down my barns and build larger ones, and there I will store all my grain and my goods.

19. And I will say to my soul, Soul, you have ample goods laid up for many years; relax, eat, drink, be merry.'

20. But God said to him, 'Fool! This night your soul is required of you, and the things you have prepared, whose will they be?'

21. So is the one who lays up treasure for himself and is not rich toward God."

Isn't it easy for us to attribute our success in life to our brilliancy? Our ingenuity, intelligence and creative gifts? How often do we show or want to show that we have it figured out and have made it all by ourselves?

In the text above, Jesus, who knows the thoughts of all the people he created told the story. In the narrative, Jesus did not give credit to the farmer that he had worked very hard, or has done some extraordinary thing, neither did Jesus attribute anything specifically to him that should distinguish him from any other farmer in the area. Instead, Jesus gave the credit of the increase to the fertile ground which produced plentifully, (Luke 12:16). The land was fertile; it produced beyond expectations, beyond what was provided for. Should we call it good luck in this farm because of a remarkably plentiful year of success? He was not thinking about bigger barns before this huge increase, but now he is. He was not thinking

94

about retirement before the surprise surplus, but now he is. He took God's act of kindness and favor for granted.

The farmer had a storage problem. Jesus allowed us to know what was going on in his thoughts. It was a soliloquy, which means he was talking to himself; making plans how to solve his surplus problem. Read his soliloquy in verses 18-20. Note the frequency of the personal pronoun "I will", which appeared four times. Note also the frequency of "My" which appeared five times. We could from his thoughts, revealed to us by Jesus, conclude that he was indeed a lonely, selfish man. Selfish, because he shut everyone out of his thoughts including God who blessed him. The Bible says in verse 17 that, "he thought within himself". He was preoccupied with his possessions, he did not take counsel or discuss with anyone, he did not pray to God about it. His thoughts were fixed on amassing and maximizing his wealth. Then keep it, relax, eat, drink, and be merry.

The farmer in our story did not think about throwing a party and inviting friends to celebrate with him. He did not think about helping the poor or employing the jobless in the community. He did not think of investing some of the money or embarking on some worthy project which could benefit others. The more men have the more they want to keep what they have and add to it. God knows the thoughts of our heart and intents. He observes what we think within ourselves and we are accountable to Him for it.

God interrupted the rich farmer's retirement plan, first, by calling him a "fool", second, God said, "This night your soul is required of you", in verse 20. The rich farmer died before he could begin to build bigger barns and enjoy what will be stored in them. Responsible planning is good. We are in this story, challenged to think beyond this temporary existence. Think about ways to be rich towards God. What about faith, obedience and service to our neighbors and others?

The word "fool" was used two times in Luke's gospel but about seventy times in Proverbs alone. The word "fool" refers to people who live their lives as if God does not exist. The fool hath said in his heart, there is no God (Psalm 14:1). Psalm 62:10 says, "If riches increased, do not set your heart on them." Proverbs 11:28 says, "Those who trust in their riches will wither, but the righteous will flourish like green leaves."

"FOOLS" There are more contemporary fools today than in Jesus' days. Let us take a brief glimpse at the long but endless lines of contemporary rich and famous fools. Do you remember MC Hammer? The young man Hammer was said to have earned more than $33 Millions in the early nineties. He reportedly spent the money on a $12 Million mansion with gold plated gates, two helicopters, and a fleet of seventeen vehicles and extravagant parties. After being bankrupt, he sold the rights of his songs to raise money. [http:// en.wikipedia.org/MC...Hammer]

You will probably remember former Philippines First Lady, Imelda Marcos. She reportedly had over a thousand pair of shoes, 888 handbags, 71 pairs of sun glasses, 508 gowns, 15 mink coats, 65 parasols. I am sure you will remember the boxer Mike Tyson, Tyson was said to have earned over $300 millions from boxing career. He lost all on cars, jewels and filed for bankruptcy. (https://answers.yahoo.com/question/index?qid)

It is apparent that the rich farmer in this narrative was operating on assumption rather than reality. He did not even know himself; that is why he thought:

- The crops were his;

- Many years belong to him;

- Things will provide for his soul;

- His life consisted in the abundance of possessions;

- He failed to realize that his body was mortal;

- Riches do not satisfy the soul;

- He did not consider the needs of others;

- He did not glorify God;

- He shut everyone else out of his mind

- A writer once called him, "A lonely, selfish atheist."

APPLYING THE PARABLE
1. Those who accumulate treasures minus God are like this man.
2. Plans for the future minus God are foolish plans.
3. Good story for reflection for those planning for retirement.

How can I be rich in this life, and also be rich toward God?
Being in Christ is the first requirement (Ephesians 2:4-7; 1:3)
Proper view or use of material possessions is an additional help (Luke 12:33-34).
(a)   Jesus said, "Sell what you have and give alms
(b)   Helping the poor is often connected with laying up treasures in heaven.
(c)   In Matthew 19:21, Jesus counseled the rich young ruler
(d)   In 1Timothy 6:17, Paul told Timothy to instruct the rich in this present world.
As we use material wealth to help others, we become rich toward God. We

99

must, however, understand that we cannot "BUY" our way into heaven.

CHARACTERISTICS OF FOOLS IN THE BIBLE
Atheism
Psalm 53:1. *The **fool** hath said in his heart, there is no God.*
Slander
Proverbs 10:18. *He that hideth hatred with lying lips, and he that uttereth a slander, is a **fool**.*
Mocking at sin
Proverbs 14:9. ***Fools** make a mock at sin: but among the righteous there is favour.*
Despising instruction
Proverbs 15:5. *A **fool** despiseth his father's instruction: but he that regardeth reproof is prudent.*
Contentiousness
Proverbs 18:6. *A **fool's** lips enter into contention, and his mouth calleth for strokes.*
Meddlesomeness
Proverbs 20:3. *It is an honour for a man to cease from strife: but every **fool** will be meddling.*
Self-confidence

Proverbs 28:26. *He that trusteth in his own heart is a **fool**: but whoso walketh wisely, he shall be delivered.*
Dishonesty
Jeremiah 17:11. *As the partridge sitteth on eggs, and hatcheth them not; so he that getteth riches, and not by right, shall leave them in the midst of his days, and at his end shall be a **fool**.*
Hypocrisy
Luke 11:39. *And the Lord said unto him, now do ye Pharisees make clean the outside of the cup and the platter; but your inward part is full of ravening and wickedness.*
Luke 11:40. *Ye **fools**, did not he that made that which is without make that which is within also?*

"What shall I do?" (Verse 17). This is a common perplexity of the rich; they often do not know what to do with their surplus wealth, though the needs of humanity call for it. "Take thine ease, eat, drink, be merry" (19). To attempt to satisfy the human soul with food, drink, merriment is pure foolishness. Human soul demands heavenly food. The rich farmer in our story does not know how to be fed spiritually because he was wrapped up in himself.

HOW WILL YOU BE REMEMBERED?

As I write today about the foolishness of a wealthy, lonely man who shuts everyone else out of his life, I have asked myself the question about how I will want those that I will one day leave behind to remember and talk about me when I am gone. I was reminded of a story I once read on the internet, written by Jennifer Rosenberg. It was the story of a man called Alfred Nobel.

In 1888, the story goes; Alfred read his obituary in a French Newspaper. It was a journalistic mistake. Alfred's brother Ludvig had died, and a careless journalist used a pre-written obituary of a wrong man. Alfred was shocked and disturbed to learn the way the world remembered him as a dynamite king, "merchant of death" who amasses wealth through the sale of explosives. Whereas he previously thought that his inventions would be useful to people and nations; alas! he was viewed as someone who dealt in blood and war for profit. Alfred did not want to go down in history with such a horrible epitaph.

Alfred then decided to show the world the true purpose of his life. He revised his will so that his fortune would be dedicated to the recognition of great, creative achievements. The highest award was to go to those who had done the most for world peace. Then his image began to change. Today, more than a century now, his name is associated with the Nobel Peace Prize. What would people and God remember about you? (http://www.nobel.se).

A Reflection on Life - James 4:13-16

13. Come now, you who say, "Today or tomorrow we will go into such and such a town and spend a year there and trade and make a profit"--
14. Yet you do not know what tomorrow will bring. What is your life? For you are a mist that appears for a little time and then vanishes.

103

15. Instead you ought to say,
"If the Lord wills, we will live
and do this or that."
16. As it is, you boast in your
arrogance. All such boasting is
evil.

Does a man's life lie in his abilities, energy, effort, training, employment, etc.? Is man capable of handling his own life? Does anybody know what will happen tomorrow? (Earthquake, fire, plane crash, death in the family, good news, bad news, tornadoes?)

If you are using King James Bible, James 4:13 opening words are, "Go to now," In today's language it means, "Come on now you who are strutting around like you own this place." He was addressing those who had a plan, place, a period, a program and a purpose that is minus God.

- The man read about in verse 13 has already planned his days (today or tomorrow)

- Planned the city of his choice (to such and such a city)

- Planned the duration of stay (spend a year)

- Planned to stay and work (buy and sell)

- Planned to make a profit (make a profit)

- How can this man be sure he will leave today or tomorrow?

- How can he be sure to reach the city he was planning to go to?

- He might have an accident, be robbed or develop an illness

- How can he be sure he will spend a year, while something can intrude his plan, (family illness)?

How can he be sure of making a profit? He may lose everything, business may fail. It is not the quest of this book to present future planning, set measurable, achievable goals as unwise, ungodly and evil. Instead, it is the author's pursuit to show that making plans for college, job, family, vacation or retirement is relevant and appropriate, but that no planning should be at the expense of one's soul or eternity. In Acts 15:36; 18:20-21 and 1Corinthians 16:5-9 we read about Apostle Paul making plans about the journey he would be going on. Reading the Epistle of James 4:13-16 we should be able to glean the important information that there are right and wrong ways of planning our work and future here on earth and I will like to write about the two ways.

"If the Lord wills." Means that man was made to be dependent upon God for all things. Do you make your plans contingent upon God's approval? Paul said in Acts 18:21 "God willing," and in 1Corinthans 16:7 he said, "If the Lord permits". When we operate this way we are showing our trust and dependence on God.

One of the wrong ways of planning is to exclude God and live our lives like He does not exist. We were required to read a book while I was in the Theological School which has the caption, "GOD IS DEAD." Some people do act as if God is dead, inactive, silent. God, the creator of this universe is alive, active and well.

In the Epistle of James 4:13-16, the pastor tried to teach his congregation about the right and wrong ways of making future plans. In verse 13, James shows that life is complex. There are the complexities of time, today, tomorrow, next week, next month etc. There are also the complexities of activities, buy, sell, build etc. Above all, there are the complexities of making daily decisions, right decisions, wrong decisions etc. As a result of these complexities none of us has a guarantee of tomorrow or what will happen. In view of these, verse 14a declares life as uncertain. Life is not only uncertain it is frail (14b).

Has the Scriptures not warned us in Proverbs 27:1, "Boast not thyself of tomorrow; for thou knowest not what a day may bring forth." The Bible has presented us several reasons why anyone of us should not boast of the next day. Here are a few of them:

Brevity of life limits knowledge
For we *are but of* yesterday, and know nothing, because our days upon earth *are* a shadow (Job 8:9; Psalm 73:22).
The future is hidden

For he knoweth not that which shall be: for who can tell him when it shall be? (Ecclesiastes 8: 7).

Coming Evils are unforeseen

For man also knoweth not his time: as the fishes that are taken in an evil net, and as the birds that are caught in the snare; so *are* the sons of men snared in an evil time, when it falleth suddenly upon them. (Ecclesiastes 9: 12).

Life is full of mysteries

As thou knowest not what *is* the way of the spirit, *nor* how the bones *do grow* in the womb of her that is with child: even so thou knowest not the works of God who maketh all. (Ecclesiastes 11:5).

Nature and Grace are also full of mysteries

The wind bloweth where it listeth, and thou hearest the sound thereof, but canst not tell whence it cometh, and whither it goeth: so is every one that is born of the Spirit. (John 3:8).

The Shepherd then asked, "What is your life?"

There are various definitions of life by the Bible writers:

David says in 1Chronicles 29:15, "Our days on earth, are as a shadow"

Job says in Job 7:7 "Remember that my life is wind"
The Psalmist says in Psalm 39:5 ..."thou has made my days as a handbreath"
The Psalmist again in Psalm 102:3 says, "For my days are consumed like smoke"..

As he began to answer his own questions, James defines life as, "a vapor" or "a shadow". Compare Psalm 39:5-6, 11. How substantial or durable is a shadow or vapor? A vapor or fog is never permanent, neither is life permanent. How quickly we succumb to sickness or accident is an illustration of our frailty. For this reason it will be foolishness to assume that we have the strength and capabilities within ourselves to make our plans. James reminds his audience that life is "brief" (14c). "It appears for a little time" like a fog or vapor.

Job also has observation about life, (Job 9:25-26;14: 1).
Other Bible writers expressed their thoughts about life in the following ways:

The Psalmist says life is like a hand breath
Psalm 39:5. Behold, thou hast made my days *as* an handbreadth; and mine age *is* as nothing before thee: verily every man at his best state *is* altogether vanity. Selah.

Isaiah says life is like a weaver's web
Isaiah 38:12. Mine age is departed, and is removed from me as a shepherd's tent: I have cut off like a weaver my life: he will cut me off with pining sickness: from day *even* to night wilt thou make an end of me.

Job says life is like a hurrying messenger
Job 9:25. Now my days are swifter than a post: they flee away, they see no good.

David says life is like a shadow
1Chronicles 29:15. For we *are* strangers before thee, and sojourners, as *were* all our fathers: our days on the earth *are* as a shadow, and *there is* none abiding.

In James 4:16a the Pastor tried to show that planning without taking into consideration whether it aligns with God's will or approval is to set ourselves up above God, he calls it arrogance and boasting which is evil. We should all agree with James and other Bible writers on this subject that life is uncertain, frail and brief. I think Solomon was right when he said, "Boast not thyself of tomorrow; for thou knowest not what a day may bring forth." (Proverbs 27:1).

Do you know that man is made to be dependent on God for life? (James 4:15a).
Do you know that every breath is a gift from God? (Daniel 5:23).
Do you know that life, breath, health, provision was a gift from God? (Acts 17:25).
Do you know that in Him we live, move, and have our being? (Acts 17:28)
Do you know that God formed man out of the dust of the ground, breathed into his nostrils, only then that man became a living being? (Genesis 2:7).
Do you know that our abilities, talents, and gifts rest in God's hands?
Do you know that death knows no holidays, birthdays or special days?
It is foolishness to plan without God. The Bible has the following to say on the subject of being a fool or foolishness:

Psalm 53:1. "The fool says in his heart, "There is no God."
Proverbs 1:7. "fools despise wisdom and instruction."

Chasing of the wind

Some of God's children have material success, live in beautifully furnished fine mansions, (and there is nothing wrong with that), others ride in beautiful expensive cars (there is nothing wrong with that either) but eventually we all find out just like King Solomon that it never satisfies. King Solomon as we shall see tried sensual pleasure, money, fame, knowledge – everything that can appeal to man in life, his conclusion was, "vanity of vanities, all is vanity". (Ecclesiastes 1:2).

Eccl 2:1-24.

> *I said in mine heart, Go to now, I*
> *will prove thee with mirth,*
> *therefore enjoy pleasure:*
> *and, behold, this also is*
> *vanity.*
> *2. I said of laughter, It is mad:*
> *and of mirth, what doeth it?*
> *3. I sought in mine heart to give*
> *myself unto wine, yet*
> *acquainting mine heart with*

wisdom; and to lay hold on folly, till I might see what was that good for the sons of men, which they should do under the heaven all the days of their life.

4. I made me great works; I builded me houses; I planted me vineyards:

5. I made me gardens and orchards, and I planted trees in them of all kind of fruits:

6. I made me pools of water, to water therewith the wood that bringeth forth trees:

7. I got me servants and maidens, and had servants born in my house; also I had great possessions of great and small cattle above all that were in Jerusalem before me:

8. I gathered me also silver and gold, and the peculiar treasure of kings and of the provinces: I gat me men singers and women singers, and the delights of the sons of men, as musical instruments, and that of all sorts.

9. *So I was great, and increased more than all that were before me in Jerusalem: also my wisdom remained with me.*

10. *And whatsoever mine eyes desired I kept not from them, I withheld not my heart from any joy; for my heart rejoiced in all my labour: and this was my portion of all my labour.*

11. *Then I looked on all the works that my hands had wrought, and on the labour that I had laboured to do: and, behold, all was vanity and vexation of spirit, and there was no profit under the sun.*

12. *And I turned myself to behold wisdom, and madness, and folly: for what can the man do that cometh after the king? Even that which hath been already done.*

13. *Then I saw that wisdom excelleth folly, as far as light excelleth darkness.*

14. *The wise man's eyes are in his head; but the fool walketh in darkness: and I myself*

perceived also that one event happeneth to them all.

15. *Then said I in my heart, as it happeneth to the fool, so it happeneth even to me; and why was I then more wise? Then I said in my heart, that this also is vanity.*

16. *For there is no remembrance of the wise more than of the fool for ever; seeing that which now is in the days to come shall all be forgotten. And how dieth the wise man? As the fool.*

17. *Therefore I hated life; because the work that is wrought under the sun is grievous unto me: for all is vanity and vexation of spirit.*

18. *Yea, I hated all my labour which I had taken under the sun: because I should leave it unto the man that shall be after me.*

19. *And who knoweth whether he shall be a wise man or a fool? Yet shall he have rule over all my labour wherein I have laboured, and wherein I have*

shewed myself wise under the sun. This is also vanity.

20. Therefore I went about to cause my heart to despair of all the labour which I took under the sun.

21. For there is a man whose labour is in wisdom, and in knowledge, and in equity; yet to a man that hath not laboured therein shall he leave it for his portion. This also is vanity and a great evil.

22. For what hath man of all his labour, and of the vexation of his heart, wherein he hath laboured under the sun?

23. For all his days are sorrows, and his travail grief; yea, his heart taketh not rest in the night. This is also vanity.

24. There is nothing better for a man, than that he should eat and drink, and that he should make his soul enjoy good in his labour. This also I saw, that it was from the hand of God.

25. For who can eat, or who else can hasten hereunto, more than I?
26. For God giveth to a man that is good in his sight wisdom, and knowledge, and joy: but to the sinner he giveth travail, to gather and to heap up, that he may give to him that is good before God. This also is vanity and vexation of spirit.

King Solomon, according to his own testimony in the above passage, pursued pleasure, undertook great projects, bought slaves, had herds and flocks, amassed wealth, acquired singers, had concubines, built houses, a temple, a Kingdom, a family (1Kings Chapters 3-11). None of these things brought him satisfaction.

King Solomon looked at those things which he had worked hard for and accomplished, he said, "It was chasing after the wind" (Ecclesiastes 2:11). Why will Solomon make that conclusion? I believe he has now understood that life has no meaning if the purposes and goals of life's activities do not lead us to

117

the pursuit of God. That is why in Psalm 27:1 he said, "Except the LORD build the house, they labour in vain that build it: except the LORD keep the city, the watchman waketh *but* in vain."

We feel the wind as it passes by, we cannot catch or keep it. All our accomplishments, big ones, small ones, good feelings about them remained temporary. Security and self-worth do not matter moments after the cessation of life.

In this chapter of the scriptures, Solomon showed very clearly that hard-work do not necessarily produce lasting fruit to those who work solely to earn money and gain possessions. Why? Because everything will be left behind at death to those who did nothing to earn it, and who may not well care for it, and all that was gained may be lost. Solomon's son who inherited his throne (1Kings 12) was a proof as he showed foolishness and lost part of the Kingdom. Hard work, serving God, taking responsibilities of those under our care will be rewarded. Hard work to glorify self will be passed to those who

may lose or spoil it all. That kind of toil
often lead to grief.

Chapter Ten

WHY WE SHOULD GO TO CHURCH

1. Going to church was a divine command in Deuteronomy 12:5 "Out of the territory of all your tribes the LORD will choose the one place where the people are to come into his presence and worship him." (GNB) Deuteronomy 16:16

2. Going to church is the third commandment. It has two purposes. One, "remember the Sabbath day to keep it holy". In Leviticus 23:3, it was a day of rest, and also a day of Sacred Assembly. You take a break from work to give your body a rest and rejuvenation for next week. It was also a day to assemble together for the purpose of corporate worship. If you are absent from church you are not keeping the Sabbath holy. Hebrews 10:25 reinforced the third commandment when the writer says that we should not forsake the assembly of ourselves as it is the manner of some. To neglect

church service is to give up encouragement and help of other Christians. We gather together to share our faith and to strengthen one another in the Lord.

3. The church is a place where to receive instructions, Micah 4:2 and their people will say, "Let us go up the hill of the LORD, to the temple of Israel's God. He will teach us what he wants us to do; we will walk in the paths he has chosen. For the LORD's teaching comes from Jerusalem; from Zion he speaks to his people.

4. Going to church carries pronounced blessings, Psalm 84:4; 122:4 how happy are those who live in your Temple, always singing praise to you.

5. The church is a place of refuge in times of trouble, Isaiah 37:1, 14. As soon as King Hezekiah heard their report, he tore his clothes in grief, put on sackcloth, and went to the Temple of the LORD.

The church provides comfort in old age, Luke 2:36-37. Anna, a prophet, was also there. She was a descendant of Phanuel from the tribe of Asher. She was now very old. Her husband had died seven years after they were married,

37. And she had been a widow for 84 years. Anna never left the temple courtyard but worshipped day and night by fasting and praying. (GW).

6. We go to church to worship God. The word "worship" comes from 2 Anglo Saxon words, **weorth** and **scipe**, when you put the two together it means, "the act of letting someone know how much they are worth to us." So, when you come to church, you are, by your presence saying how much God is worth to you. If you are absent from church, you are loudly saying God is not worth much to you. What are your excuses for not coming?

7. In Matthew 18:20 Jesus himself said, "Where two or three have come together in my name, I am

there among them." Every time we gather together before Him he is there to bless, answer prayers, and to serve our interest. Now, tell me, why will you not be in church? "For in His presence is fullness of joy" Psalm 16:11.

EXAMPLES OF GOING TO CHURCH

Examples from Christ, Luke 4:16; *Then Jesus came to Nazareth, where he had been brought up. As usual he went into the synagogue on the day of worship. He stood up to read the lesson.* (GW) Luke 18:10.

John 7:14; *The festival was nearly half over when Jesus went to the Temple and began teaching.* (GNB).

Luke 18:10. *Once there were two men who went up to the Temple to pray: one was a Pharisee, the other a tax collector.* (GNB) Luke 24: 52-53 John, 7:14.

Examples from the Apostles
Acts 2:46; *Day after day they met as a group in the Temple, and they had their*

meals together in their homes, eating with glad and humble hearts, (GNB)

Act 3:1. *One day Peter and John went to the Temple at three o'clock in the afternoon, the hour for prayer.*

MORE ABOUT WHY WE GO TO CHURCH

Hebrews 10:25. *Not forsaking the assembling of ourselves together, as the custom of some is, but exhorting one another; and so much the more, as ye see the day drawing nigh.*

Matthew 28:20. *Teaching them to observe all things whatsoever I commanded you: and lo, I am with you always, even unto the end of the world.* (ASV).

Exodus 20:8. *Remember the Sabbath day, to keep it holy.* (ASV).

Hebrews 10:24. *And let us consider one another to provoke unto love and good works;* (ASV).

Acts 2:42. *And they continued stedfastly in the apostles' teaching and fellowship, in the breaking of bread and the prayers.*

Proverbs 27:17. *Iron sharpeneth iron; so a man sharpeneth the countenance of his friend.*

Hebrews 3:13. *But exhort one another day by day, so long as it is called To-day; lest anyone of you be hardened by the deceitfulness of sin:*

> Psa. 133:1-3. *A Song of Ascents; of David. Behold, how good and how pleasant it is for brethren to dwell together in unity!*
> *2. It is like the precious oil upon the head, that ran down upon the beard, Even Aaron's beard; that came down upon the skirt of his garments;*
> *3. Like the dew of Hermon, That cometh down upon the mountains of Zion: For there Jehovah commanded the blessing, Even life for evermore.* (ASV).

Psalm 84:10. *For a day in thy courts is better than a thousand. I had rather be a doorkeeper in the house of my God, than to dwell in the tents of wickedness.* (ASV).

2Timothy 3:16. *Every scripture inspired of God is also profitable for teaching, for reproof, for correction, for instruction which is in righteousness.*

Matthew 16:18. *And I also say unto thee, that thou art Peter, and upon this rock I will build my church; and the gates of Hades shall not prevail against it.* (ASV).

Romans 12:1. *I beseech you therefore, brethren, by the mercies of God, to present your bodies a living sacrifice, holy, acceptable to God, which is your spiritual service.*

Mathew 18:19. *Again I say unto you, that if two of you shall agree on earth as touching anything that they shall ask, it shall be done for them of my Father who is in heaven.* (ASV).

1Corinthians 12:12. *For as the body is one, and hath many members, and all the members of the body, being many, are one body; so also is Christ.* (ASV).

Psa. 11:2-7. For, lo, the wicked bend the bow, they make ready their arrow upon the string, that they may shoot in darkness at the upright in heart;

3. If the foundations be destroyed, what can the righteous do?

4. Jehovah is in his holy temple; Jehovah, his throne is in heaven; His eyes behold, his eyelids try, the children of men.

5. Jehovah trieth the righteous; but the wicked and him that loveth violence his soul hateth.

6. Upon the wicked he will rain snares; Fire and brimstone and burning wind shall be the portion of their cup.

7. For Jehovah is righteous; He loveth righteousness: The upright shall behold his face.

Psalm 27:4. *One thing have I asked of Jehovah, that will I seek after; that I may dwell in the house of Jehovah all the days of my life, to behold the beauty of Jehovah, And to inquire in his temple.* (ASV).

I read the following article from an e-mail sent to me and it blessed me, hope it blesses you too.

NO MORE EXCUSES:
The day Zacchaeus climbed the tree, short people lost their right to use HEIGHT as an excuse. The day David killed Goliath, young people lost their right to use AGE as an excuse. The day Joseph became Prime Minster, illegal immigrants lost their right to use STATUS as an excuse. The day the

woman with the issue of blood used her last strength to touch the helm of Jesus' garment, weak people lost their right to use WEAKNESS as an excuse. The day the widow dropped her offering, poor people lost their right to use POVERTY as an excuse. The day Daniel met the lions, fearful people lost their right to use DEATH as an excuse. The day grace came through Christ, the "LOST" lost their right to use SIN as an excuse. NO MORE EXCUSES.

Reading this book, you should gain insight into these questions:

- What is life?
- Does a man's life lie in his abilities, energy, training, etc.?
- Was man created to be self or God's dependent for life?
- Who is a fool?
- Does death recognize birthdays, holidays and special days?
- Does man know what will happen tomorrow?
- How can I prepare for tomorrow?

ABOUT THE AUTHOR

Reverend Samuel A. Abegunde, was born in Obbo-Aiyegunle, Ekiti Local Government of Kwara State, Nigeria. After graduating from Nigerian Premier College in Yaba Lagos, he worked as secretary of Free Gospel Society of Nigeria, 96 Palm Avenue Street/ 126, Isolo Road, Mushin, Lagos. Reverend Abegunde resigned from the secretarial job in order to devote his time fully as resident pastor of Gospel Mission Assembly, at Number 2, Salawu Street in Osodi, Lagos State, Nigeria.

Reverend Abegunde was elected Chairman of Osodi Evangelistic Crusade (O.E.C), for two terms a position he held until his departure to the U.S.A. in April 1980. He studied Theology at Saint Joseph's University in Philadelphia and Villanova University Graduate School, Villanova, PA. Reverend Abegunde also obtained a Master's degree in Education at Holy Family University in Philadelphia.

Reverend Abegunde was the first pastor of Christ Apostolic Church

(C.A.C) in Philadelphia. He returned to Nigeria in December 1985 to resume his pastoral leadership in Gospel Mission Assembly. He served as the first Pastor-General of Liberty Evangelical Church during its inception in January 1986. He is currently General Overseer Emeritus of Liberty Evangelical Church worldwide.

Reverend Abegunde authored several books including, *"Integrity In Ministry"*, *"Hiring Shepherds, not Hirelings"* *"Why Are You Alone?" The Quiet Life of Isaac"* *"From Gilgal to Jordan" and "The Wounded Man"* He is married to Pastor (Mrs.) Bernice Abegunde. They are blessed with children.

ISBN 978-0-9886615-6-1